# DAY HIKES AROUND
# MISSOULA
## MONTANA

## INCLUDING THE BITTERROOTS
## AND THE SEELEY-SWAN VALLEY

**by Robert Stone**

Photographs by Robert Stone
Published by Day Hike Books, Inc.
114 South Hauser  Box 865  Red Lodge, MT 59068
Design: Paula Doherty
Library of Congress Catalog Card Number: 97-74949
© 1998

# TABLE OF CONTENTS

## THE HIKES

### In and Around Missoula

### West of Missoula and Fish Creek Drainage

## Bitterroot Mountains

## Seeley—Swan Valley

## Rock Creek Drainage and Welcome Creek

# About Missoula and the Hikes

Missoula, the third largest city in Montana, is an active, picturesque university town. The town was first settled in the 1860s. It grew rapidly as a mining and logging center with the arrival of the railroad. Missoula has a beautiful historic commercial district with turn-of-the-century architecture. Near the university is Missoula's historic residential area. The University of Montana, on the banks of the Clark Fork River, is located near the base of Mount Sentinel by the mouth of Hellgate Canyon. Missoula is rich in character and diversity with a wide variety of museums, art galleries, boutiques, restaurants, musical and cultural events.

At an elevation of 3,205 feet and surrounded by mountains, Missoula sits at the hub of five merging valleys—the Bitterroot from the south, the Mission from the north, the Blackfoot and Hellgate from the east and the Missoula from the west. Three rivers—the Bitterroot, the Blackfoot and the Clark Fork—are in or within a few miles of the city. A short distance in any direction leads to national forests and wilderness areas.

Missoula is surrounded by the two-million-acre Lolo National Forest. The Lolo National Forest has an abundance of wildlife, including black bear, moose, deer, big horn sheep, mountain goats and elk. The forest also has 350,000 acres of winter elk range. The land is rich with ponderosa pine, lodgepole pine, Douglas fir, subalpine fir and western larch. The Lolo National Forest provides access into four wilderness areas and a variety of recreational areas. Four miles southeast of Missoula is the Pattee Canyon Recreational Area. Two miles southwest is the Blue Mountain Recreational Area. Less than four miles north is the Rattlesnake National Recreational Area. Much of the area is set aside for preservation as wilderness.

Rattlesnake Creek, Missoula's watershed, flows through

the canyon's narrow valley floor. The drainage is fed by more than fifty smaller creeks. Within this area are eight different trailheads with a network of interconnecting trails. The trails follow a variety of creeks and gulches through alpine and subalpine landscape. The glacially carved topography is home to 7,000-foot summits, hanging valleys, cirques and more than thirty lakes.

To the south of Missoula, along Highway 93, is the Bitterroot Valley. The Bitterroot River carved this twenty-mile wide valley that sits at an elevation of 3,000 feet. This fertile valley is nestled between two mountain ranges—the Bitterroot Mountains and the Sapphire Mountains. To the west are the dramatic Bitterroot Mountains. The Bitterroots straddle the Continental Divide and form the Montana/Idaho border. The northern portion of the Bitterroots is among Montana's wettest areas, receiving more than 100 inches of moisture annually. The Bitterroot Range is known for its jagged 9,000-foot granite peaks and deep canyons. Each of the fourteen canyons are also creek drainages with headwaters from alpine lakes. These precipitous canyon walls rise 5,000 feet from the valley floor in only three miles. The Bitterroot National Forest encompasses 1.6 million acres, with about half the forest as protected wilderness area. The Bitterroot Mountains have an extensive 1,600-mile trail system, including the Nez Perce Trail, route of the tragic flight in 1877, and the historic Lewis and Clark Trail.

To the east of the Bitterroot Valley are the molten slopes of the Sapphire Mountains. The wild Sapphire Range has 98,000 acres of designated wilderness, including the Welcome Creek Wilderness. With narrow canyons and steep ridges, the main artery of the Welcome Creek Wilderness is Rock Creek, a "blue ribbon" rated trout fishing creek.

To the northeast of Missoula, on Highway 83, is the glacially carved Seeley-Swan Valley. This ten-mile wide corridor extends for eighty miles with two beautiful rivers—the Clearwater River flowing into the Blackfoot River and the Swan River flowing into Flathead Lake. The valley is bordered to the west for thirty miles by the majestic, snow-capped Mission Mountains. To the valley's east is the Swan Mountain Range, offering access into the Bob Marshall Wilderness, the Scapegoat Wilderness and the Great Bear Wilderness. Along the valley and its bordering mountain ranges are hundreds of pristine lakes. With over 400 miles of hiking trails, dozens of campgrounds, resorts, guest ranches and easy access to the back country, the Seeley-Swan Valley is a recreational haven.

This guide focuses on 26 hikes of various lengths around Missoula. The hikes have been chosen for their outstanding beauty and variety. Most of these hikes require easy to moderate effort unless otherwise noted. Each hike has its own description, driving and hiking directions, plus an adjoining map. The trails are also detailed on an assortment of commercial maps, including the U.S. Geological Survey topographical maps, the U.S. Forest Service Selway-Bitterroot National Forest map, the Lolo National Forest map and the Trails Missoula booklet. The relevant maps are listed with each hike and can be purchased at most area sporting goods stores.

As for attire and equipment, hiking shoes offer the best support and are preferable for all of these hikes. The elevation for these hikes can be as high as 8,000 feet. At this altitude the air can be cool. Afternoon thundershowers are common throughout the summer. Be prepared for unpredictable weather by wearing layered clothing and packing a warm hat. A rain poncho, sunscreen, mosquito repellent and drinking water are recommended. Pack a lunch and enjoy a picnic at scenic outlooks, creeks, rivers, lakes or wherever you find the best spot.

Enjoy your hike!

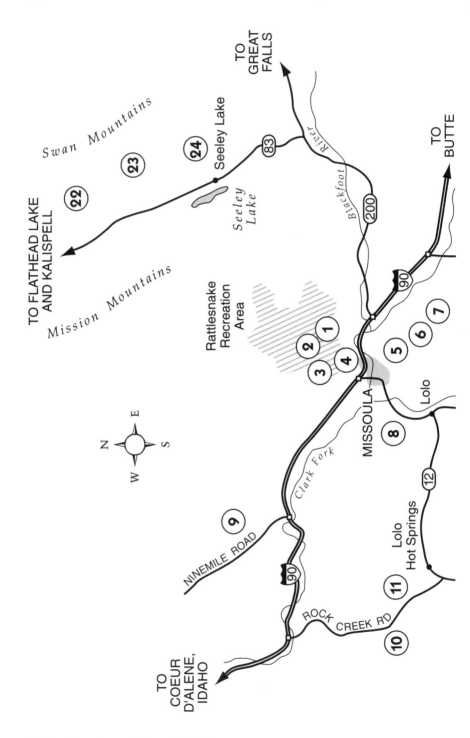

# MAP OF THE HIKES

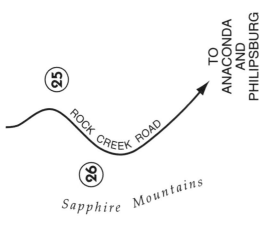

25

ROCK CREEK ROAD

TO
ANACONDA
AND
PHILIPSBURG

26

*Sapphire* Mountains

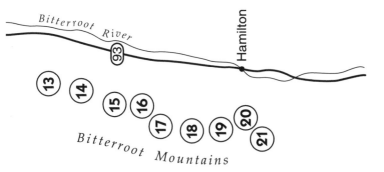

*Bitterroot River*

93

Hamilton

13 14 15 16 17 18 19 20 21

*Bitterroot* Mountains

12

LOLO PASS
TO IDAHO

# Hike 1
## Main Rattlesnake Trail
## Rattlesnake National Recreation Area

**Hiking distance:** 6 miles round trip
**Hiking time:** 3 hours
**Elevation gain:** 400 feet
**Topo:** U.S.G.S. Northeast Missoula
Rattlesnake Nat'l. Recreation Area and Wilderness map

**Summary of hike:** The 61,000-acre Rattlesnake National Recreation Area, part of the Lolo National Forest, is located at the northern city limits of Missoula. This spectacular area has sweeping mountains, hanging valleys, lake-filled basins and a large variety of orchids. There are eight separate trailheads, providing access to a web of interconnecting trails. The Main Rattlesnake Trail parallels Rattlesnake Creek up the main corridor of the glacially carved drainage basin.

**Driving directions:** In Missoula, take Van Buren Street north, which turns into Rattlesnake Drive. Drive 4.1 miles north from I-90 to Sawmill Gulch Road on the left. Turn left, crossing over Rattlesnake Creek, and continue 0.2 miles to the main trail parking lot on the right.

**Hiking directions:** Follow the main trail north, past the trailhead sign. At a half mile is a junction with the Stuart Peak Trail on the left (Hike 2) and a bridge over Rattlesnake Creek on the right. Continue straight ahead on the main trail another quarter mile, and take the smaller path to the right. This path stays close to the creek and reconnects with the main trail 1.7 miles from the trailhead. Continue following the main trail up canyon. At 2 miles, take the posted Wallman Trail to the left. Along the way are two trail forks. Take the right forks, rejoining the main trail. Return along the main trail, completing a double loop. To hike further, continue up canyon another half mile, descending into Poe Meadow.

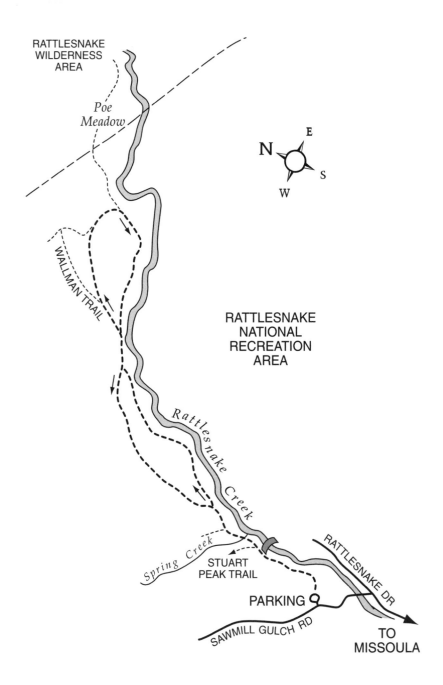

RATTLESNAKE
WILDERNESS
AREA

*Poe
Meadow*

N E S W

WALLMAN TRAIL

RATTLESNAKE
NATIONAL
RECREATION
AREA

*Rattlesnake Creek*

*Spring Creek*

STUART
PEAK TRAIL

RATTLESNAKE DR

PARKING

SAWMILL GULCH RD

TO
MISSOULA

# MAIN RATTLESNAKE TRAIL

# Hike 2
## Spring Creek Loop
### Rattlesnake National Recreation Area

**Hiking distance:** 5.5 mile loop
**Hiking time:** 3 hours
**Elevation gain:** 450 feet
**Topo:** U.S.G.S. Northeast Missoula
Rattlesnake Nat'l. Recreation Area and Wilderness map
Trails Missoula map

**Summary of hike:** The Stuart Peak Trail heads up Spring Gulch parallel to Spring Creek. The Spring Creek Loop follows old cow paths and a farm lane, looping around both sides of the creek. Spring Creek empties into Rattlesnake Creek, a municipal watershed for Missoula.

**Driving directions:** In Missoula, take Van Buren Street north, which turns into Rattlesnake Drive. Drive 4.1 miles north from I-90 to Sawmill Gulch Road on the left. Turn left, crossing over Rattlesnake Creek, and continue 0.2 miles to the main trail parking lot on the right.

**Hiking directions:** From the parking lot, hike north past the trailhead signs. Take the Main Rattlesnake Trail (Hike 1) up the valley a half mile to the Stuart Peak Trail junction on the left. To the right is a bridge crossing over Rattlesnake Creek. Take the narrower Stuart Peak Trail heading upstream alongside Spring Creek. At the 1.3 mile marker is a log crossing over Spring Creek to the right for a shorter 2.6-mile loop. Continue north, up Spring Gulch, passing the Curry Gulch Trail on the left. At 2.7 miles, as Spring Gulch narrows, is another trail junction. The left fork continues up the canyon to Stuart Peak. Take the right fork, and cross a small wooden bridge over Spring Creek. Head downstream back to the Rattlesnake's main corridor, completing the loop. Take the trail to the right back to the trailhead.

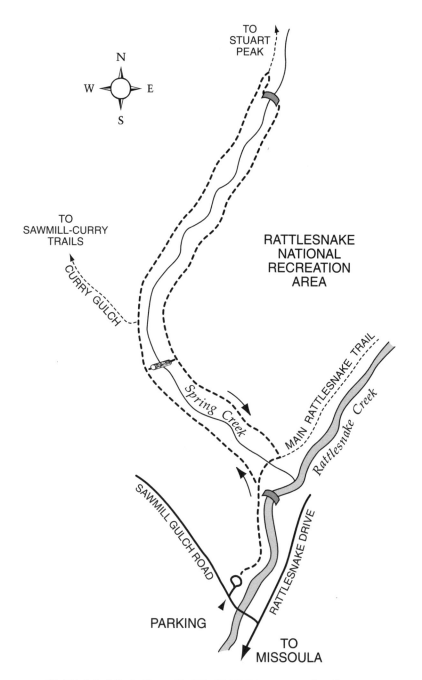

N W E S

TO STUART PEAK

TO SAWMILL-CURRY TRAILS

CURRY GULCH

RATTLESNAKE NATIONAL RECREATION AREA

Spring Creek

MAIN RATTLESNAKE TRAIL

Rattlesnake Creek

SAWMILL GULCH ROAD

RATTLESNAKE DRIVE

PARKING

TO MISSOULA

# SPRING CREEK LOOP

# Hike 3
## Sawmill Gulch Loop
### Rattlesnake National Recreation Area

**Hiking distance:** 2.6 mile loop
**Hiking time:** 1.5 hours
**Elevation gain:** 500 feet
**Topo:** U.S.G.S. Northeast Missoula
Rattlesnake Nat'l. Recreation Area and Wilderness map

**Summary of hike:** Sawmill Gulch, part of the Curry Trail System, is a more recent addition (acquired in 1986) to the Rattlesnake National Recreation Area. The trails are quieter and less frequented than the Main Rattlesnake corridor. Many of these trails were originally made in the 1800s by prospectors, settlers and livestock. This trail follows a large meadow, passing remnants of the original ranch buildings. The Curry Trail System connects with the Spring Creek Trail (Hike 2).

**Driving directions:** In Missoula, take Van Buren Street north, which turns into Rattlesnake Drive. Drive 4.1 miles north from I-90 to Sawmill Gulch Road on the left. Turn left, crossing over Rattlesnake Creek, and continue 1.4 miles to the trailhead parking area at road's end. (At 1.2 miles is a road fork—stay to the right.)

**Hiking directions:** From the parking area, pass the gate and hike north towards the meadow. The trail follows the eastern edge of the meadow up the draw. Near the top, the remnants of the old ranch buildings are on the right. Just past the ranch site is a junction. Take the right fork up a narrow draw to a second junction. The left fork continues deeper into the Curry Trail System. Take the right fork uphill along the eastern cliff edge, overlooking the meadow below. The trail winds through the forest to another junction. Again, take the right fork. The trail curves right and descends back to the meadow, completing the loop. Head left, back to the trailhead.

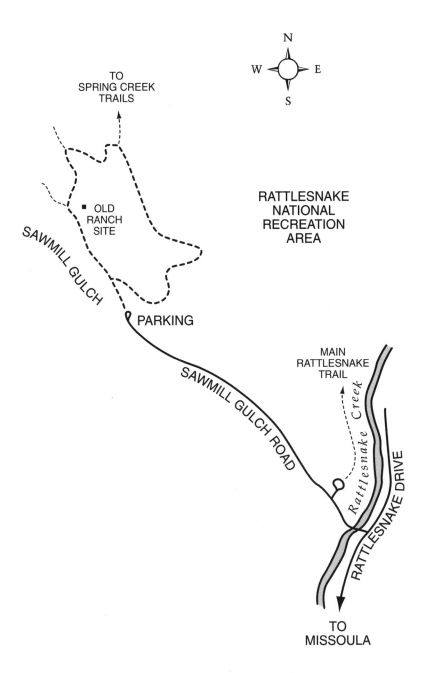

# SAWMILL GULCH LOOP

# Hike 4
## Bolle Birdwatching Trail
## Greenough Park

**Hiking distance:** 1 mile loop
**Hiking time:** 30 minutes
**Elevation gain:** Level
**Topo:** U.S.G.S. Northeast Missoula
  Trails Missoula booklet

**Summary of hike:** Greenough Park has hiking paths that wind along Rattlesnake Creek as it flows through this 42-acre park at the mouth of the Rattlesnake Valley. The park is a bird habitat donated to the City of Missoula in 1902 by the Greenough Family. The gift included a provision that the land would be "forever maintained in its natural state." Several information stations about birds are located along the path. As many as 120 varieties of birds have been known to inhabit the area. Greenough Park has mature ponderosa pine trees, cottonwoods and lush riparian vegetation along Rattlesnake Creek. Benches and picnic tables are available.

**Driving directions:** In Missoula, take Van Buren Street north. Drive 0.3 miles north from I-90 to Locust Street on the left. Turn left, and continue 2 blocks to Monroe Street. The parking lot is on the west side of Monroe Street.

**Hiking directions:** From the parking lot, head to the bridge over Rattlesnake Creek. Once over the bridge, take the path to the right, hiking clockwise around the loop. To the left is a short loop around a grassy picnic area by the creek. The trail along the west side of Rattlesnake Creek is paved. At 0.4 miles, the trail crosses over the creek via a bridge to a foot trail on the right. The return trail is a natural path through a shady forest on the east bank of the creek. The trail follows Rattlesnake Creek back to the parking lot.

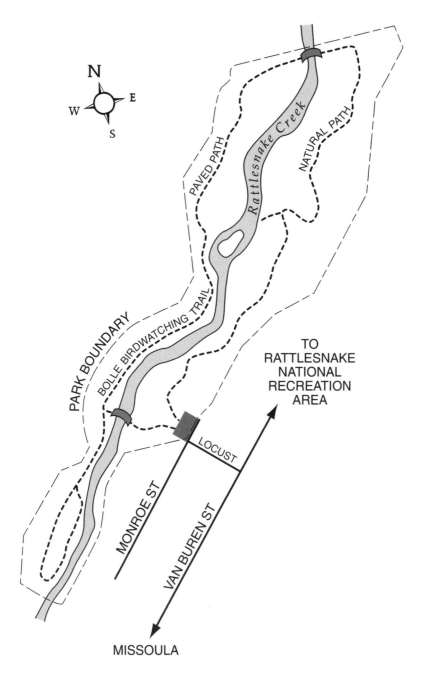

N
W E
S

PAVED PATH

*Rattlesnake Creek*

NATURAL PATH

PARK BOUNDARY

BOLLE BIRDWATCHING TRAIL

TO
RATTLESNAKE
NATIONAL
RECREATION
AREA

LOCUST

MONROE ST

VAN BUREN ST

MISSOULA

# GREENOUGH PARK

# Hike 5
# Hellgate Canyon-Mount Sentinel Loop

**Hiking distance:** 6 mile loop
**Hiking time:** 3 hours
**Elevation gain:** 1,950 feet
**Topo:**  U.S.G.S. Southeast Missoula
Trails Missoula booklet

**Summary of hike:** The hike up Hellgate Canyon begins by the University of Montana along the Kim Williams Nature Trail, an abandoned railroad bed on the banks of the Clark Fork River. The trail climbs 2.5 miles up the forested north face of Hellgate Canyon, gaining 1,600 feet before the final ascent of Mount Sentinel at 5,160 feet. From the top, the entire Missoula Valley area is within view.

**Driving directions:** Park south of the Clark Fork River by the University of Montana, one block east of Maurice Avenue. During the school year, this parking lot is usually full. If so, park near Van Buren Street north of the Clark Fork River. Cross the Van Buren footbridge over the river by Jacobs Island Park.

**Hiking directions:** Begin along the Kim Williams Nature Trail heading east, parallel to the Clark Fork River. At one mile is a junction with the Hellgate Canyon Trail on the right. Take this trail up the switchbacks. The well-groomed trail is not steep, but it goes steadily uphill. The higher you climb, the more dynamic the views. At 3.5 miles—the top of the canyon—is a junction with the Crazy Canyon Trail (Hike 6). Take a sharp right for the final quarter mile ascent to the top of Mount Sentinel. The trail crisscrosses its way to the top. After resting, relaxing and taking in the views, follow the path one mile down the west face of Mount Sentinel to the "M." From here, the trail zigzags down to the university. At the bottom, head to the right, towards the Clark Fork River and the trailhead.

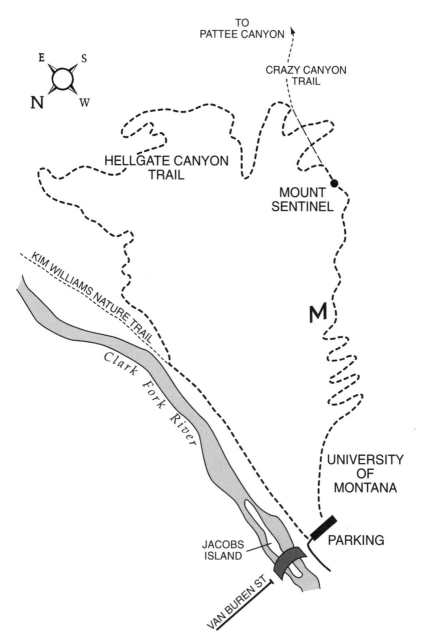

TO
PATTEE CANYON

CRAZY CANYON
TRAIL

E    S

N    W

HELLGATE CANYON
TRAIL

MOUNT
SENTINEL

KIM WILLIAMS NATURE TRAIL

Clark Fork River

M

UNIVERSITY
OF
MONTANA

PARKING

JACOBS
ISLAND

VAN BUREN ST.

# HELLGATE CANYON–
# MOUNT SENTINEL LOOP

# Hike 6
## Crazy Canyon Trail to Mount Sentinel
## Pattee Canyon Recreation Area

**Hiking distance:** 7 miles round trip
**Hiking time:** 3.5 hours
**Elevation gain:** 1,150 feet
**Topo:** U.S.G.S. Southeast Missoula
Trails Missoula booklet

**Summary of hike:** The Crazy Canyon Trail begins in the Pattee Canyon Recreation Area. The trail follows a road through Crazy Canyon in the Lolo Forest to the summit of Mount Sentinel, the 5,160-foot peak above the University of Montana. From Mount Sentinel are 360-degree views of the surrounding mountains and the entire Missoula Valley. For a one-way, 5.5-mile hike, leave a shuttle car by the university.

**Driving directions:** From downtown Missoula, drive 2 miles south on Higgins Avenue to Pattee Canyon Road and turn left. Continue 3.4 miles to the Crazy Canyon trailhead parking lot on the left.

**Hiking directions:** From the parking lot, the trail begins to the north. Take the right fork uphill through the forest to a vehicle restricted road. Take the road to the left. The trail follows the road most of the way. Stay on the road rather than veering off on the various footpaths. At 1.7 miles, the trail crosses Crazy Canyon curving to the left (west). At three miles is a junction with the Hellgate Canyon Trail (Hike 5). Leave the road, taking the footpath towards Mount Sentinel. The footpath switchbacks up the ridge crossing the road several times before rejoining it for the final ascent. After savoring the views, return by retracing your steps. If there is a shuttle car at the university, begin the 1.75-mile descent, passing the "M" on the way down.

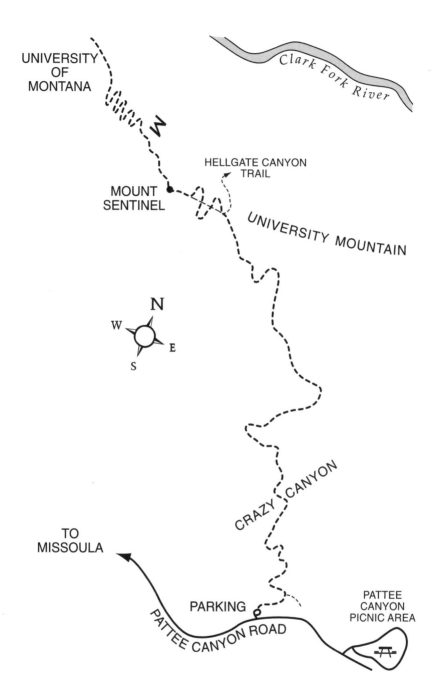

UNIVERSITY
OF
MONTANA

*Clark Fork River*

HELLGATE CANYON
TRAIL

MOUNT
SENTINEL

UNIVERSITY MOUNTAIN

N
W        E
S

CRAZY CANYON

TO
MISSOULA

PARKING

PATTEE CANYON ROAD

PATTEE
CANYON
PICNIC AREA

# CRAZY CANYON TRAIL

# Hike 7
## Sam Braxton National Recreation Trail
## Pattee Canyon Recreation Area

**Hiking distance:** 3.4 mile loop
**Hiking time:** 1.5 hours
**Elevation gain:** 350 feet
**Topo:** U.S.G.S. Southeast Missoula
Trails Missoula booklet

**Summary of hike:** The Sam Braxton Trail is located in the Pattee Canyon Recreation Area, four miles southeast of Missoula. The trail is a winding, curving trail, looping through a forest of large, old growth western larch and ponderosa pine trees. In the winter, Pattee Canyon is a popular cross-country ski area with natural and groomed trails.

**Driving directions:** From downtown Missoula, drive 2 miles south on Higgins Avenue to Pattee Canyon Road and turn left. Continue 4.2 miles to the Sam Braxton trailhead parking lot on the right.

**Hiking directions:** From the parking lot, hike south past the gate to the posted trailhead. Bear to the right 0.1 mile to a junction. Take the posted Sam Braxton Recreational Trail to the left, winding gently uphill. The trail winds through the forest like a maze. At times it will seem confusing due to old logging paths that cross through the area. At any of the unmarked junctions, follow the direction arrows or the National Recreation Trail insignia on the trees. When you least expect it, the trail completes the loop back to the trailhead.

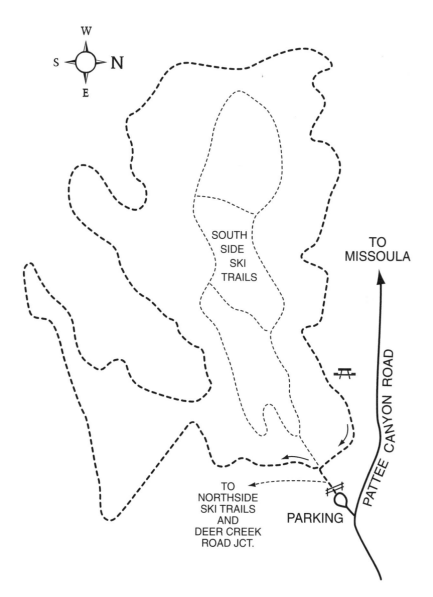

# SAM BRAXTON
# NATIONAL RECREATION
# TRAIL

# Hike 8
## Maclay Flat Trail
## Blue Mountain Recreation Area

**Hiking distance:** 1.25 or 1.8 mile loop
**Hiking time:** 1 hour
**Elevation gain:** Level
**Topo:** U.S.G.S. Southwest Missoula
Trails Missoula booklet

**Summary of hike:** The Maclay Flat Nature Trail in the 5,500-acre Blue Mountain Recreation Area, part of the Lolo National Forest, is located only two miles southwest of Missoula. The trail borders the Bitterroot River and the Big Flat Irrigation Ditch on the return. The irrigation ditch is used by farms and ranches through Big Flat before emptying into the Clark Fork River. The wide, level interpretive trail loops through a riparian forest rich with aspen, cottonwood, ponderosa pine trees and meadows. There are sixteen information sites that describe the geology, river system, vegetation and wildlife in the area. Benches and picnic tables are available along the wheelchair accessible trail.

**Driving directions:** From Missoula, drive 2 miles south of Reserve Street on Highway 93 to Blue Mountain Road and turn right. Continue 1.7 miles to the Maclay Flat parking lot on the right.

**Hiking directions:** From the parking lot, the well-defined trail heads east. Take the left fork, hiking clockwise. At 0.3 miles the trail parallels the banks of the Bitterroot River. At 0.6 miles is the junction with the cutoff trail. The right fork shortens the hike to a 1.25-mile loop. Continue straight ahead for the 1.8-mile loop. The trail curves south and returns back to the trailhead along the north edge of the Big Flat Irrigation Ditch.

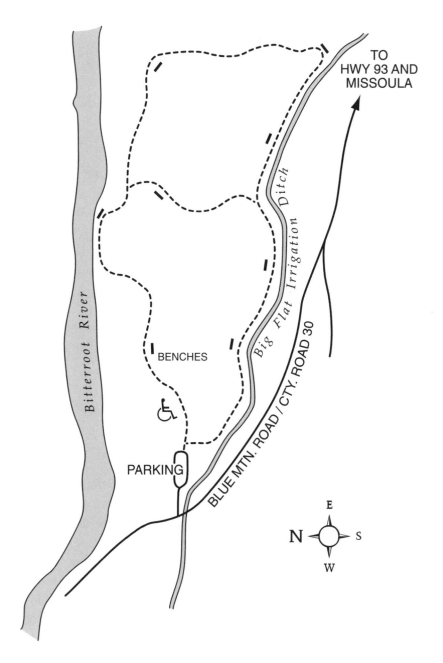

# MACLAY FLAT TRAIL

# Hike 9
# Grand Menard Discovery Trail

**Hiking distance:** 1.5 mile loop
**Hiking time:** 1 hour
**Elevation gain:** 150 feet
**Topo:** Lolo National Forest Grand Menard Discovery Trail map

**Summary of hike:** Located in the Lolo National Forest, the Grand Menard Discovery Trail is an interpretive trail in the Ninemile Valley. The rambling nature trail has two loops that wind through a ponderosa pine and Douglas fir forest. The inner, shorter loop is wheelchair accessible. From the trail are views of Stark Mountain and the fire lookout at 7,350 feet. An interpretive brochure is available at the trailhead and at the Ninemile Ranger Station.

**Driving directions:** Drive 21 miles west on I-90 to the Ninemile Road/Exit 82. Turn right (north) and drive 1.4 miles to Remount Road and turn right. Continue 3.5 miles, passing the historic ranger station, to the Grand Menard turnoff and turn left. Drive 0.2 miles to the parking lot on the left. Turn in and curve left to the trailhead.

**Hiking directions:** The trail heads south from the end of the parking lot, past the interpretive trail sign. At the first trail junction, take the fork to the right. A short distance ahead is a bridge crossing over a stream. Continue to the next fork and again take the trail to the right. The trail crosses another bridge to the west side of the loop. The trail heads south overlooking a large meadow and pasture to the west. Returning back towards the trailhead are two more bridge crossings before completing the loop. Take the trail to the right, and return to the parking lot.

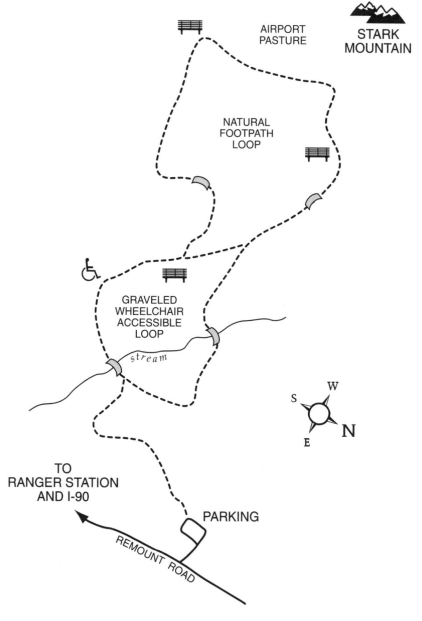

AIRPORT
PASTURE

STARK
MOUNTAIN

NATURAL
FOOTPATH
LOOP

GRAVELED
WHEELCHAIR
ACCESSIBLE
LOOP

stream

W
S
E
N

TO
RANGER STATION
AND I-90

PARKING

REMOUNT ROAD

# GRAND MENARD
# DISCOVERY TRAIL

# Hike 10
# Cache Creek Trail

**Hiking distance:** 6 to 10 miles round trip
**Hiking time:** 3 to 5 hours
**Elevation gain:** 500 feet
**Topo:** U.S.G.S. White Mountain

**Summary of hike:** The Cache Creek Trail is located in the Fish Creek drainage, part of the Lolo National Forest. The trail parallels Cache Creek through a portion of the famous 1910 fire, known as the "Great Burn." The fire spread from Washington to Montana. Evidence of the fire is still apparent. This area is a winter range for wildlife and a fall hunting ground. The drainage gains little elevation for nine miles before ascending Cache Saddle.

**Driving directions:** From Missoula, drive 8 miles south on Highway 93 to Lolo. Take Highway 12 heading west for 25.8 miles to Fish Creek Road on the right, less than one mile beyond Lolo Hot Springs. Turn right and drive 11.2 miles to Montana Creek Road and turn left. Continue 0.6 miles, crossing the South Fork of Fish Creek, to a road fork. Take the left fork 0.7 miles to the trailhead parking area at road's end.

From I-90, drive 38 miles west of Missoula to the Fish Creek exit. Drive south 20 miles to Montana Creek Road on the right.

**Hiking directions:** From the parking area, the trail heads west, past the Forest Service information board. The trail begins high above Cache Creek. The wide drainage offers frequent views of White Mountain. At 0.3 miles is a shallow but wide crossing of Montana Creek. To keep dry, there is a log crossing 20 yards downstream. A narrow path leads to the crossing. After crossing, take the trail to the left. The trail approaches the shore of Cache Creek, then strays along the hillside to a second stream crossing at 1.2 miles. The trail leads for many miles into the canyon. Choose your own turnaround spot.

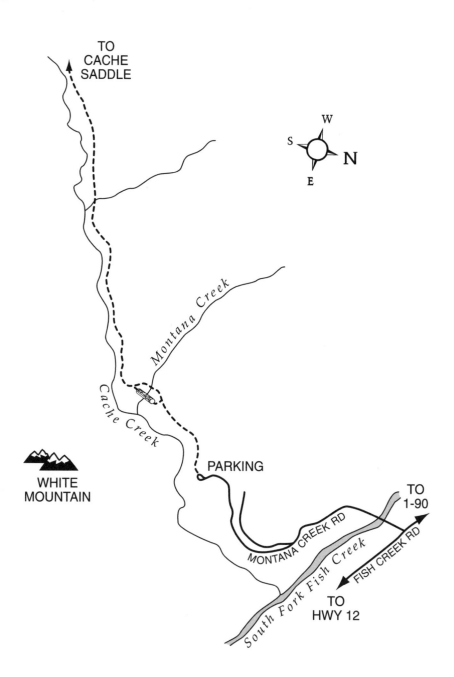

# CACHE CREEK TRAIL

# Hike 11
# Burdette Creek Trail

**Hiking distance:** 6 to 10 miles round trip
**Hiking time:** 3 to 5 hours
**Elevation gain:** 400 feet
**Topo:** U.S.G.S. Lupine Creek

**Summary of hike:** The Burdette Creek Trail, located in the Lolo National Forest, provides access into the drainage for five miles, then deadends. The trail follows Burdette Creek through meadows and an old growth forest. Known as an excellent wildlife winter range, Burdette Creek is primarily used in the fall during hunting season. The canyon gains only 400 feet in five miles. There are three walk-through creek crossings.

**Driving directions:** From Missoula, drive 8 miles south on Highway 93 to Lolo. Take Highway 12 heading west for 25.8 miles to Fish Creek Road on the right, less than one mile beyond Lolo Hot Springs. Turn right and drive 9 miles to the Burdette Creek trailhead on the right. (Stay on Road 343, the middle road, at a 3-way junction.) Parking pullouts are on the left.

From I-90, drive 38 miles west of Missoula to the Fish Creek exit. Drive south 22 miles to the Burdette Creek trailhead on the left.

**Hiking directions:** The trail begins one mile southeast of Burdette Creek. Hike up the forested draw and over the ridge on an old abandoned road heading north. At the top of the hill, the road fades. Watch for the footpath veering off to the left. As the trail descends 300 feet, there are great views of the drainage and Burdette Creek below. At one mile, the trail crosses Burdette Creek. After crossing, the trail heads northeast up the wide drainage. At 2.5 miles, as the canyon narrows, is a second creek crossing. At 3 miles, the trail crosses back again to the west side of the creek. For a six-mile hike, this is a good turnaround spot. For a ten-mile hike, continue as the canyon narrows and curves east. The trail crosses talus fields and passes beaver ponds to the trail's end. Return along the same path.

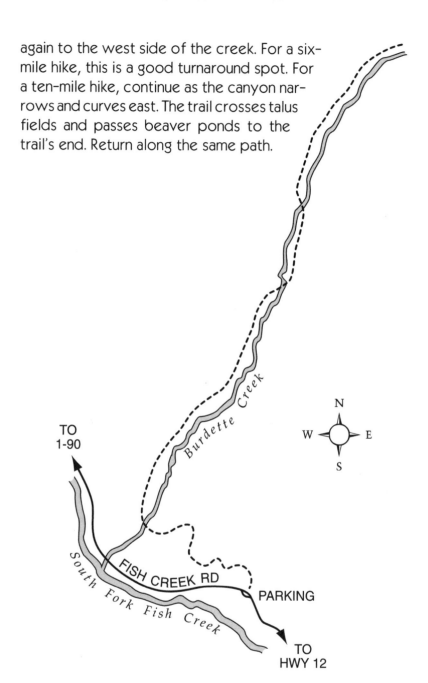

# BURDETTE CREEK TRAIL

# Hike 12
# Lee Creek Interpretive Trail

**Hiking distance:** 2.5 mile loop
**Hiking time:** 1.5 hours
**Elevation gain:** 200 feet
**Topo:** Lolo National Forest Lee Creek Interpretive Trail map

**Summary of hike:** Don't let the words "interpretive trail" deter you from this hike. It is a fascinating and informative trail. The hike introduces you to ponderosa pine, lodgepole pine and Douglas fir trees. Then it demonstrates, with examples, the effects of logging, lightening, fire, birds, decay and deterioration upon these trees. An interpretive brochure is available at the trailhead and at the Forest Service Visitor Centers.

**Driving directions:** From Missoula, drive 8 miles south on Highway 93 to Lolo. Take Highway 12 heading west for 26.5 miles to the Lee Creek Campground on the left. The campground is located 1.3 miles west of Lolo Hot Springs. Turn left, then take a quick right to the parking lot.

**Hiking directions:** The trailhead is in the campground. From the parking lot, walk up the main road 100 yards to the road fork veering left. The trail heads left along the hillside into a lodgepole pine forest. The trail continues up through the forest to twenty information sites. From the top, the trail winds back down to a stream and bridge crossing. The interpretive trail ends at the gravel road. Head down the gravel road to the right back to the parking lot.

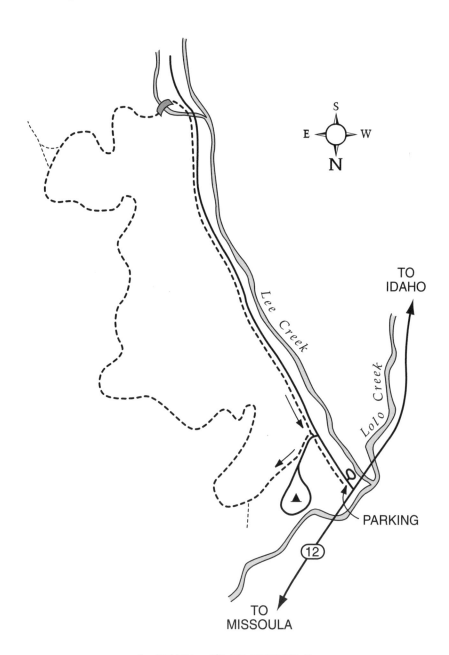

S
E — W
N

TO
IDAHO

Lee Creek

LoLo Creek

PARKING

(12)

TO
MISSOULA

# LEE CREEK
# INTERPRETIVE TRAIL

# Hike 13
# Bass Creek Trail

**Hiking distance:** 3 miles round trip
**Hiking time:** 1.5 hours
**Elevation gain:** 500 feet
**Topo:** U.S.G.S. Saint Mary Peak and Saint Joseph Peak
　　　　 U.S.F.S. Selway Bitterroot Wilderness map

**Summary of hike:** The Bass Creek Trail is an easy hike that gains elevation gradually. The trail parallels the continuous series of whitewater cascades, small waterfalls and pools of Bass Creek. This hike takes in the beginning portion of the trail, heading west 1.5 miles into the canyon to an old log dam. Behind the dam is a large, clear pond. For an overnight trip, continue up the Bass Creek Trail an additional 5.5 miles to Bass Lake, gaining 3,000 feet en route.

**Driving directions:** From Missoula, drive 20 miles south on Highway 93 to the Bass Creek Road on the right. Turn right and continue 2.5 miles to the trailhead parking area at road's end.
　　　From Hamilton, drive 23 miles north on Highway 93 to Bass Creek Road on the left.

**Hiking directions:** The Bass Creek Trail immediately enters the forested canyon on an old vehicle-restricted road. One hundred yards up the road, the trail forks left and stays close to the creek. For the first half mile, large boulders covered with moss and lichen border the trail while Bass Creek cascades down canyon on your left. Then the trail climbs high above the creek along the hillside. As you near the dam, the trail approaches the creek again. Narrow side paths to the left lead down to the log dam. To return, take the same trail back.

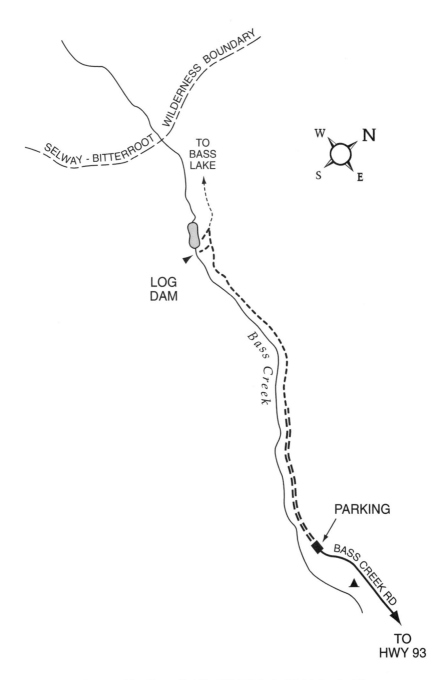

SELWAY - BITTERROOT

WILDERNESS BOUNDARY

TO
BASS
LAKE

W N S E

LOG
DAM

Bass Creek

PARKING

BASS CREEK RD

TO
HWY 93

# BASS CREEK TRAIL

# Hike 14
# Kootenai Creek Trail

**Hiking distance:** 6 miles round trip
**Hiking time:** 3 hours
**Elevation gain:** 600 feet
**Topo:** U.S.G.S. Saint Mary Peak and Saint Joseph Peak
U.S.F.S. Selway Bitterroot Wilderness map

**Summary of hike:** The Kootenai Creek Trail is a heavily used hiking trail for good reason. The creek puts on a dynamic display of raging whitewater, cascades and small waterfalls. The trail stays close to picturesque Kootenai Creek, winding through a narrow, steep-walled canyon. The trail eventually leads to the four Kootenai Lakes located 9 miles from the trailhead, gaining 2,600 feet in elevation.

**Driving directions:** From Missoula, drive 23 miles south on Highway 93 to the North Kootenai Creek Road on the right. The road is located one mile north of the Stevensville junction. Turn right and continue 2 miles to the trailhead parking area at road's end.
   From Hamilton, drive 20 miles north on Highway 93 to North Kootenai Creek Road on the left.

**Hiking directions:** From the parking area, hike west past the trailhead information board. The trail follows the north edge of the canyon, always in view of the tumbling Kootenai Creek. There are continuous dips and rises as you head west into the canyon, but the trail remains close to the creek. The trail enters the Selway–Bitterroot Wilderness Boundary at 2.6 miles. At 3 miles the gradient steepens. Choose your own turnaround spot.

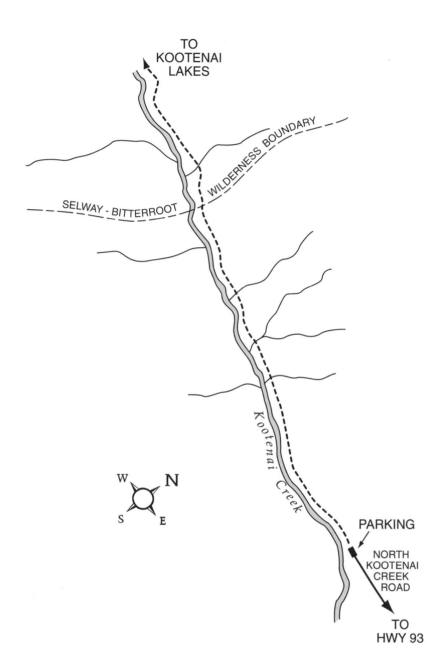

TO
KOOTENAI
LAKES

WILDERNESS BOUNDARY

SELWAY - BITTERROOT

Kootenai Creek

W N
S E

PARKING

NORTH
KOOTENAI
CREEK
ROAD

TO
HWY 93

# KOOTENAI CREEK TRAIL

# Hike 15
# Big Creek Trail

**Hiking distance:** 4 miles round trip
**Hiking time:** 2 hours
**Elevation gain:** 600 feet
**Topo:** U.S.G.S. Victor and Gash Point
U.S.F.S. Selway Bitterroot Wilderness map

**Summary of hike:** The Big Creek Trail is a popular hiking and horsepacking trail. The trail follows Big Creek for nine miles up to Big Creek Lake and dam at an elevation of 5,865 feet. It is the largest high mountain lake in the Bitterroots. This hike follows Big Creek for the first two miles of the trail. There are several white sand beaches near wide, slow moving portions of the creek. These beaches are perfect spots for having a picnic and for soaking your feet in the cool water on a hot day.

**Driving directions:** From Missoula, drive 30 miles south on Highway 93 to Bell Xing West on the right. It is located 5.6 miles south of the Stevensville turnoff. Turn right and continue 0.5 miles to Meridian Road. Turn right and follow the hiking trail signs 2.8 miles to a road split just past the old mine pit. Take the right fork 1.2 miles downhill to the Big Creek trailhead parking area.
   From Hamilton, drive 13.5 miles north on Highway 93 to Bell Xing West on the left.

**Hiking directions:** The trailhead is at the far end of the parking lot by the Forest Service information board. From here, you are immediately engulfed in the thick, shady forest. Bear to the left and cross the stream. Big Creek cascades down the canyon to the north of the trail. At one mile, the trail crosses into the Selway–Bitterroot Wilderness, then descends a short distance to Big Creek and a bridge crossing. After crossing to the north side of the creek, continue up canyon 0.3 miles to the first in a series of sand beaches. A side path on the left leads to the beach. This is a good lunch area and turnaround spot. Return along the same trail.

If you choose to hike further, the trail continues for several miles parallel to the creek to Big Creek Lake.

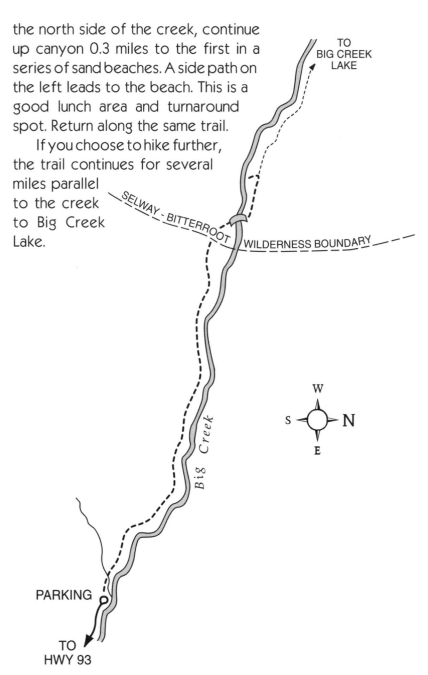

TO BIG CREEK LAKE

SELWAY - BITTERROOT

WILDERNESS BOUNDARY

W
S · N
E

Big Creek

PARKING

TO HWY 93

# BIG CREEK TRAIL

# Hike 16
# Glen Lake

**Hiking distance:** 5 miles round trip
**Hiking time:** 2.5 hours
**Elevation gain:** 700 feet
**Topo:** U.S.G.S. Gash Point
  U.S.F.S. Selway Bitterroot Wilderness map

**Summary of hike:** Glen Lake is a beautiful high mountain lake surrounded by steep, serrated cliffs. The lake sits in a bowl below these towering mountains. Rising high in the southwest is Gash Point at an elevation of 8,885 feet. The trail borders, then enters, the Selway-Bitterroot Wilderness. It is a steady uphill climb to Glen Lake.

**Driving directions:** From Missoula, drive 30 miles south on Highway 93 to Bell Xing West on the right. It is located 5.6 miles south of the Stevensville turnoff. Turn right and continue 0.5 miles to Meridian Road. Turn right and follow the hiking trail signs 2.8 miles to a road split just past the old mine pit. Take the left fork 7.6 miles up the winding road to the trailhead parking pullouts on the right.
  From Hamilton, drive 13.5 miles north on Highway 93 to Bell Xing West on the left.

**Hiking directions:** From the trailhead, it feels as though you are at the top of the mountain, but you are only near the top. Hike uphill, past the trail sign, paralleling the wilderness boundary for 1.2 miles. The trail levels out in a small burn area, then curves to the west, entering the Selway-Bitterroot Wilderness Area. The trail descends as you approach Glen Lake. A trail leads around the shoreline in both directions. You cannot circle the lake as the mountains are too steep along the north side. Return by retracing your steps. (The trail continues northwest to Hidden Lake, but the trail is steep and vague.)

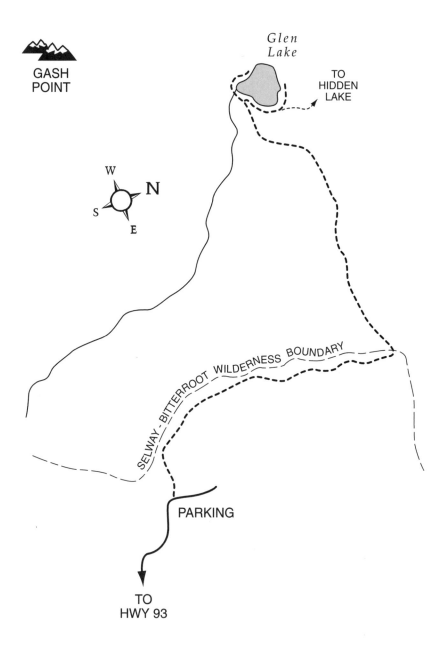

GASH
POINT

*Glen
Lake*

TO
HIDDEN
LAKE

W N
S
E

SELWAY - BITTERROOT WILDERNESS BOUNDARY

PARKING

TO
HWY 93

# GLEN LAKE

# Hike 17
# Bear Creek Trail
# to the waterfall

**Hiking distance:** 3 miles round trip
**Hiking time:** 1.5 hours
**Elevation gain:** 400 feet
**Topo:** U.S.G.S. Victor and Gash Point
U.S.F.S. Selway Bitterroot Wilderness map

**Summary of hike:** You can easily spend the day at the waterfall area in Bear Creek. It is a playground of whirlpools, cascades, slides and falls. Flat, terraced rock slabs warmed by the sun make great sunbathing and picnic spots. An easy, well-defined trail heads west through the forest to the falls.

**Driving directions:** From Missoula, drive 35 miles south on Highway 93 to the Bear Creek Road on the right. Turn right and continue 2.3 miles to Red Crow Road. Turn right and drive 0.7 miles to a road junction. Turn left and continue 3.1 miles straight ahead to the Bear Creek trailhead parking area.

From Hamilton, drive 8.5 miles north on Highway 93 to Bear Creek Road on the left.

**Hiking directions:** The clearly marked Bear Creek Trail takes off from the far end of the parking lot. Bear Creek cascades down the canyon to the north of the trail. Follow the trail through the forest, parallel to the creek. After crossing a boulder field, the trail reenters the forested canyon. There is a slight elevation gain throughout the hike. In a clearing just beyond the third boulder field is a beautiful cascade and falls. Bear Creek carves a whitewater mosaic through the rocks. This is our destination and turnaround spot.

For an overnight trip, the trail continues 8.5 miles to Bear Lake and 9.5 miles to Bear Pass.

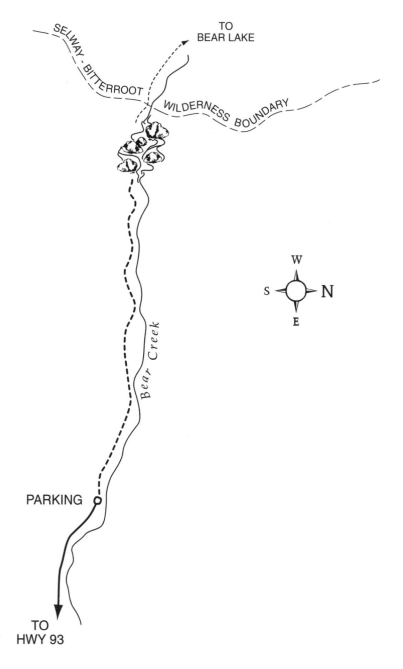

SELWAY - BITTERROOT

WILDERNESS BOUNDARY

TO
BEAR LAKE

W
S ◇ N
E

Bear Creek

PARKING

TO
HWY 93

# BEAR CREEK TRAIL

# Hike 18
# Mill Creek Trail to the waterfall

**Hiking distance:** 6 miles round trip
**Hiking time:** 3 hours
**Elevation gain:** 650 feet
**Topo:** U.S.G.S. Hamilton North and Printz Ridge
U.S.F.S. Selway Bitterroot Wilderness map

**Summary of hike:** Mill Creek is a continuous display of cascades, falls and pools. The creek originates at Mill Lake at an elevation of 6,550 feet, eleven miles from the trailhead. The Mill Creek Trail follows the rushing creek all the way to the lake. Soaring canyon walls tower above the trail. This hike takes in the first three miles of the trail to a magnificent 60-foot waterfall and a swimming hole at the base of the falls. The large boulders make perfect seats for viewing the falls and relaxing.

**Driving directions:** From Missoula, drive 39 miles south on Highway 93 to the Dutch Hill Road on the right. It is located by the flashing yellow light and a sign to Pinesdale. Turn right and continue 2.4 miles to Bowman Road. Turn left and drive 0.3 miles to the posted Mill Creek trailhead road on the right. Turn right and drive 0.8 miles to the trailhead parking area at road's end.
From Hamilton, drive 4 miles north on Highway 93 to Dutch Hill Road on the left.

**Hiking directions:** From the parking area, hike west past the information board. The trail parallels, then crosses, a small stream. Mill Creek tumbles down canyon to the north. At 0.5 miles, the trail crosses a log bridge over Mill Creek. After crossing, head left up the narrow canyon. At one mile, the canyon widens, opening up to the sky. The trail enters the Selway-Bitterroot Wilderness at 2.2 miles. At 3 miles, the trail crosses a large, flat rock slab. A hundred yards beyond the slab is Mill Creek Falls. After enjoying the falls, return along the same trail.

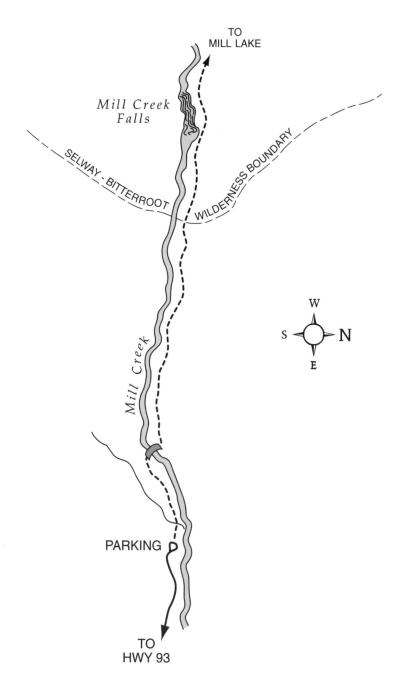

TO
MILL LAKE

*Mill Creek
Falls*

SELWAY - BITTERROOT

WILDERNESS BOUNDARY

*Mill Creek*

W
S N
E

PARKING

TO
HWY 93

# MILL CREEK TRAIL

# Hike 19
# Blodgett Canyon to the waterfall

**Hiking distance:** 7 miles round trip
**Hiking time:** 3.5 hours
**Elevation gain:** 600 feet
**Topo:** U.S.G.S. Hamilton North and Printz Ridge
U.S.F.S. Selway Bitterroot Wilderness map

**Summary of hike:** Blodgett Canyon is considered the most picturesque of the Bitterroot's many canyons. The jagged peaks of Printz Ridge to the north and Romney Ridge to the south rise nearly 4,000 feet from the canyon floor. Blodgett Creek snakes through the deep canyon. The creek alternates between wide, clear pools and turbulent whitewater cascades. The trail has an easy elevation grade and is well maintained. Although the trail leads nearly twenty miles up the canyon, this hike leads 3.5 miles to a waterfall (cover photo).

**Driving directions:** From Missoula, drive 43 miles south on Highway 93 to the town of Hamilton. Turn right on Main Street and drive 1.2 miles west to Ricketts Road on the right. Turn right and continue 0.5 miles to Blodgett Camp Road and turn left. Continue 2.4 miles to a junction with Road 736. Turn right and drive 1.5 miles to the Blodgett Creek trailhead parking area at road's end.

**Hiking directions:** From the parking area, walk back along the road, crossing to the south side of Blodgett Creek and to the trailhead on the right. There are gentle rises, falls and boulder field crossings along the trail. At 2.5 miles, the trail crosses a sturdy bridge over Blodgett Creek. Continue heading west as the trail levels out and the canyon widens. One mile past the bridge, the trail makes a short ascent to the waterfall. House-size boulders can be used to sit and picnic on. Return along the same trail.

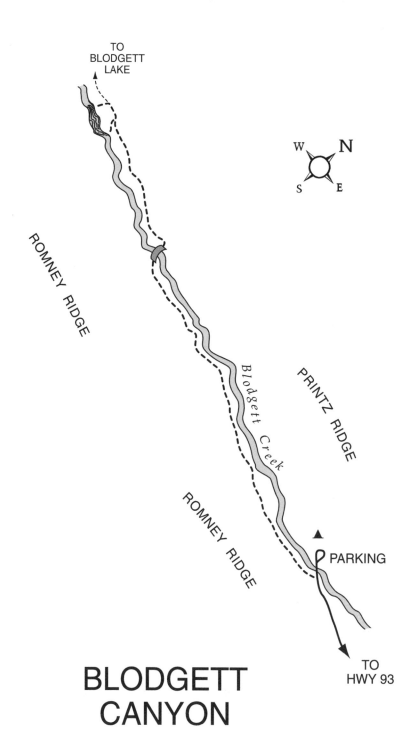

TO
BLODGETT
LAKE

N
W E
S

ROMNEY RIDGE

PRINTZ RIDGE

Blodgett Creek

ROMNEY RIDGE

PARKING

# BLODGETT
# CANYON

TO
HWY 93

# Hike 20
# Blodgett Canyon Overlook

**Hiking distance:** 3 miles round trip
**Hiking time:** 1.5 hours
**Elevation gain:** 400 feet
**Topo:**  U.S.G.S. Hamilton North
  U.S.F.S. Selway Bitterroot Wilderness map

**Summary of hike:** This stunning trail begins at Canyon Creek and leads to the north around Romney Ridge to the Blodgett Canyon Overlook. There are tremendous views throughout this hike. The hike offers views of the peaks surrounding Blodgett Canyon, the Canyon Creek drainage, the Sapphire Mountains to the east, the Bitterroot Valley and the town of Hamilton below. All of these views are afforded with very little elevation gain. Benches are also provided at the various lookout points.

**Driving directions:** From Missoula, drive 43 miles south on Highway 93 to the town of Hamilton. Turn right on Main Street and drive 1.2 miles west to Ricketts Road on the right. Turn right and continue 0.5 miles to Blodgett Camp Road and turn left. Continue 2.4 miles to a junction with Road 735. Turn left and drive 2.8 miles to the Canyon Creek trailhead parking area at road's end.

**Hiking directions:** From the parking area, hike to the west 25 yards up the Canyon Creek Trail (Hike 21) to a junction on the right. Take this unsigned trail heading north. There are several gradual switchbacks up the south and east sides of Romney Ridge. Then the trail heads north through the ponderosa pine forest to the cliffs overlooking Blodgett Canyon. At the trail's end, there are many lookout spots and ledges among the jagged peaks. Return along the same trail.

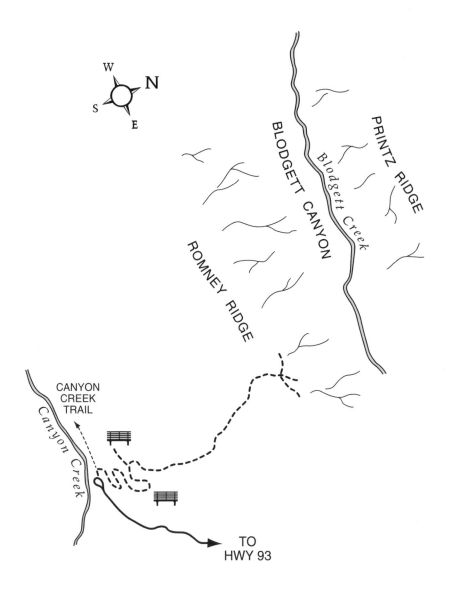

# BLODGETT CANYON
## OVERLOOK

# Hike 21
# Canyon Creek Trail

**Hiking distance:** 7 to 8 miles round trip
**Hiking time:** 3.5 to 5 hours
**Elevation gain:** 900 feet
**Topo:** U.S.G.S. Hamilton North, Printz Ridge, Ward Mountain
U.S.F.S. Selway Bitterroot Wilderness map

**Summary of hike:** The Canyon Creek Trail climbs 2,300 feet in 5.5 miles to East Lake and Canyon Lake. This hike follows the first four miles of the trail, which includes some steep scrambles. Thick tree roots reach across the trail along with stable, well-seated rocks. You can hear the creek through the deep, quiet forest but only approach its banks occasionally. Four miles from the trailhead is Canyon Falls, a long, 200-foot cascade off the rocky cliffs. The last half-mile stretch before the falls is very steep and not recommended for everyone. Just before the gradient steepens, the trail passes a small but beautiful cascade with a clear pool. For those who do not want to take on the last half mile, this is a great destination spot to enjoy.

**Driving directions:** From Missoula, drive 43 miles south on Highway 93 to the town of Hamilton. Turn right on Main Street and drive 1.2 miles west to Ricketts Road on the right. Turn right and continue 0.5 miles to Blodgett Camp Road and turn left. Continue 2.4 miles to a junction with Road 735. Turn left and drive 2.8 miles to the Canyon Creek trailhead parking area at road's end.

**Hiking directions:** From the parking area, hike west past the Forest Service information board. Throughout the hike the trail gains elevation moderately except for several short, steep sections. The trail continues through the thick forest, entering the Selway-Bitterroot Wilderness at 1.8 miles. At 3.5 miles the trail heads away from the creek and climbs steeply. Before the ascent, a side path to the left leads to the small cascade and pool. To see Canyon Falls, begin climbing for a half mile. The long cascade will become prominent as you reach the clearing. Although they are not visible from this elevation, East Lake, Canyon Lake and Wyant Lake sit above the falls.

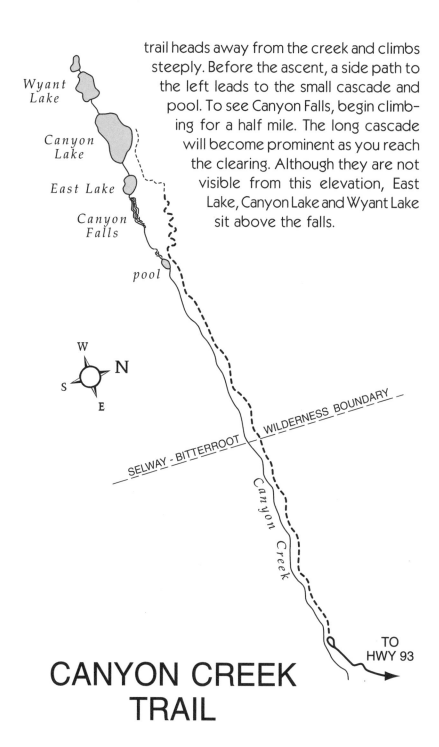

# CANYON CREEK
# TRAIL

# Hike 22
## Holland Lake and Falls

**Hiking distance:** 3 miles round trip
**Hiking time:** 2 hours
**Elevation gain:** 600 feet
**Topo:** U.S.G.S. Holland Lake

**Summary of hike:** The Holland Falls Trail, located in the Flathead National Forest, parallels the northern shore of Holland Lake to Holland Creek and Falls. Holland Falls is a beautiful and majestic waterfall. The trail leads to rock ledges, natural coves, and sitting areas ideal for resting, picnicking and viewing the waterfall. This trail is a popular access route into the Bob Marshall Wilderness, passing Upper Holland Lake en route.

**Driving directions:** From Missoula, drive 4 miles east on I-90 to Highway 200 east. Continue 33 miles to Clearwater Junction at Highway 83 and turn left. Seeley Lake is 15 miles ahead. From the town of Seeley Lake, drive 21 miles north to Holland Lake Road and turn right. Continue 3.8 miles to the trailhead parking area at the end of the road.

**Hiking directions:** From the parking area, take the sign posted trail south toward the shore of Holland Lake. Twenty yards before the shoreline, the Holland Falls Trail heads east (left), parallel to Holland Lake's northern shore. As the trail climbs and dips along the hillside, you will hike past a beautifully forested island in Holland Lake. The trail curves around to the east side of the lake, hugging the shoreline. There are four log crossings over lake inlet streams. After crossing, the trail ascends 400 feet with a series of switchbacks. As the trail climbs, the views across the lake and of the snow-streaked Mission Mountains to the west are magnificent (photo on back cover). At 1.5 miles, the trail reaches the rocky ledges overlooking Holland Falls. To return, retrace your steps.

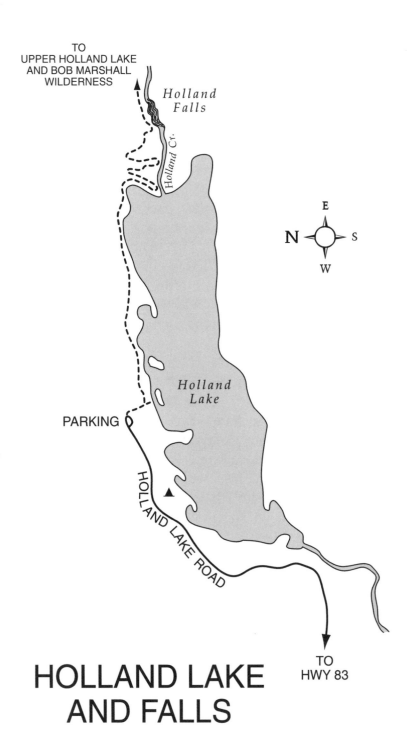

TO
UPPER HOLLAND LAKE
AND BOB MARSHALL
WILDERNESS

*Holland
Falls*

Holland Cr.

E

N ◇ S

W

*Holland
Lake*

PARKING

HOLLAND LAKE ROAD

TO
HWY 83

# HOLLAND LAKE
# AND FALLS

# Hike 23
# Clearwater Lake Loop

**Hiking distance:** 2.9 mile loop
**Hiking time:** 1.5 hours
**Elevation gain:** Near level
**Topo:** U.S.G.S. Holland Lake

**Summary of hike:** Clearwater Lake, located in the Lolo National Forest, is a rich, blue lake completely surrounded by lush, green forest. The level trail circles the perimeter of the lake. From the west shore of the lake are views of the Swan Mountain Range to the east. From the lake's south shore are views of the Mission Mountain Range to the west. Ducks and loons can frequently be spotted on the lake.

**Driving directions:** From Missoula, drive 4 miles east on I-90 to Highway 200 east. Continue 33 miles to Clearwater Junction at Highway 83 and turn left. Seeley Lake is 15 miles ahead. From the town of Seeley Lake, drive 13.6 miles north to the Clearwater Loop Road and turn right. Continue 7 miles on the winding road to the Clearwater Lake trailhead parking area on the right.

After the hike, you may return by continuing along the Clearwater Loop Road 6.2 miles further to another junction with Highway 83.

**Hiking directions:** From the parking area, the trail heads west through the forest for a short quarter mile to Clearwater Lake. As with most loop trails, you can choose the direction and return back to the same spot, completing the loop. The trail around Clearwater Lake is 2.4 miles and stays close to the shoreline with small rises and dips. Upon completing the loop, return along the trail heading back to the trailhead.

MISSION MOUNTAINS

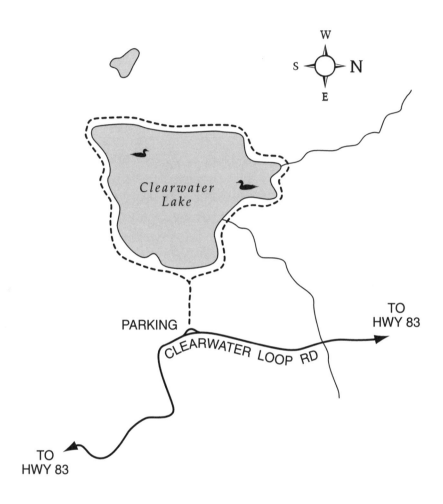

W
S — N
E

Clearwater
Lake

PARKING

TO
HWY 83

CLEARWATER LOOP RD

TO
HWY 83

SWAN MOUNTAINS

# CLEARWATER LAKE LOOP

# Hike 24
# Morrell Lake and Falls

**Hiking distance:** 5 miles round trip
**Hiking time:** 2.5 hours
**Elevation gain:** 250 feet
**Topo:** U.S.G.S. Morrell Lake

**Summary of hike:** The Morrell Falls National Recreation Trail, located at the base of the Swan Mountain Range, is among the most popular trails in the area. The rolling terrain leads through a pine, fir and spruce tree forest to Morrell Lake, where Crescent Mountain rises sharply from the eastern shore. Morrell Falls is a series of falls and steep cascades for a total 200-foot drop. From the end of the trail and base of the falls is a stunning view of the 90-foot lower falls, the largest of the drops.

**Driving directions:** From Missoula, drive 4 miles east on I-90 to Highway 200 east. Continue 33 miles to Clearwater Junction at Highway 83 and turn left. Seeley Lake is 15 miles ahead. From the town of Seeley Lake, drive less than a half mile north to Morrell Creek Road (also known as Cottonwood Lakes Road) and turn right. Continue 1.1 miles to a sign posted junction. Turn left on West Morrell Road and drive 5.6 miles to another sign posted junction and turn right. The trailhead parking area is 0.7 miles ahead, curving left en route.

**Hiking directions:** From the parking area, the well-marked trail heads east for a short distance, then curves right, heading north. The rolling, forested terrain gains little elevation. At two miles, the trail passes a pond and continues past the west shore of Morrell Lake. At the northern end of the lake is a trail fork. Take the left fork, leading away from Morrell Lake, to a bridge that crosses a lake outlet stream. From the bridge, the trail curves right to the base of Morrell Falls. Return along the same trail.

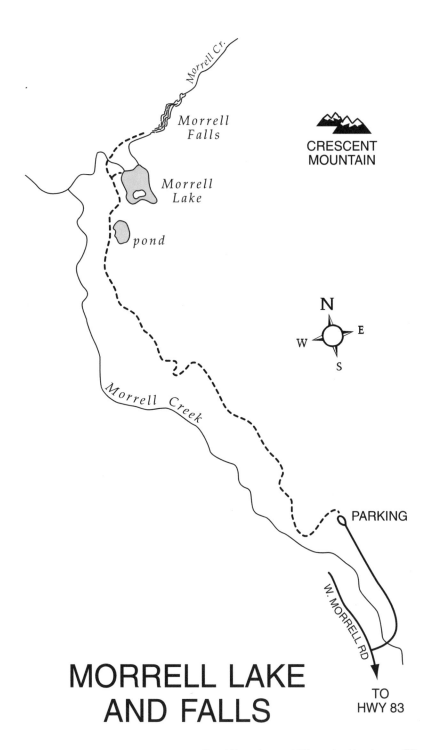

Morrell Cr.

Morrell
Falls

CRESCENT
MOUNTAIN

Morrell
Lake

pond

N

W · E

S

Morrell Creek

PARKING

W. MORRELL RD

# MORRELL LAKE
# AND FALLS

TO
HWY 83

# Hike 25
# Grizzly Creek Trail

**Hiking distance:** 3.5 miles round trip
**Hiking time:** 2 hours
**Elevation gain:** 450 feet
**Topo:** U.S.G.S. Grizzly Point and Spink Point

**Summary of hike:** The Grizzly Creek Trail is a beautiful yet seldom hiked trail. It is located in the 28,000-acre Welcome Creek Wilderness, part of the Lolo National Forest. This remote hike has a deep wilderness feel. The trail heads into the canyon, crossing Grizzly Creek several times.

**Driving directions:** From Missoula, drive 21 miles east on I-90 to the Rock Creek Road exit. Turn right and continue 11.4 miles to the Ranch Creek Road junction on the left. Turn left and drive 0.8 miles to the Grizzly Creek trailhead parking area on the left.

**Hiking directions:** From the parking area, head east past the buck fence. The trail immediately enters the mouth of Grizzly Canyon. Grizzly Creek flows down canyon to the south of the trail. The canyon begins to narrow at 0.5 miles. The first of four creek crossings is at 0.75 miles. The creek is small, but you will have to wade through it. The second crossing is at one mile. Rocks may be used to hop across. There are two additional crossings over the next 0.75 miles. The trail continues beyond the fourth crossing, but the gradient steepens. Return along the same trail.

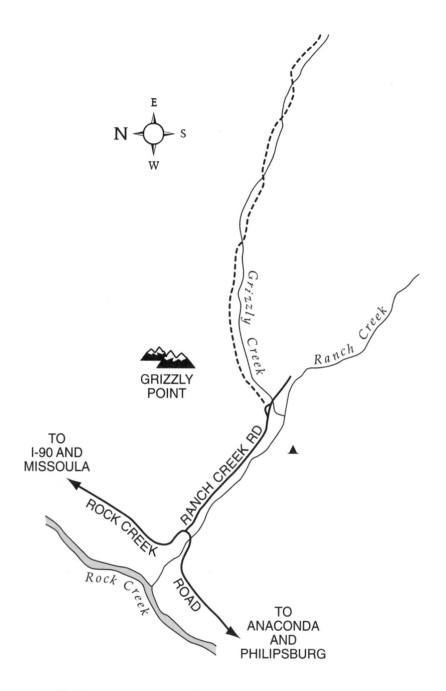

# GRIZZLY CREEK TRAIL

# Hike 26
# Welcome Creek Trail

**Hiking distance:** 5 miles round trip
**Hiking time:** 2.5 hours
**Elevation gain:** 500 feet
**Topo:** U.S.G.S. Grizzly Point and Cleveland Mountain

**Summary of hike:** The "Indiana Jones" style suspension bridge, crossing high over Rock Creek, makes the Welcome Creek Trail a hike long remembered. Below the suspension bridge is a white sand beach. The Welcome Creek Trail enters a quiet and remote, forested canyon in the Sapphire Mountains. The narrow canyon has fresh water springs, old turn-of-the-century mining ruins and log cabins.

**Driving directions:** From Missoula, drive 21 miles east on I-90 to the Rock Creek Road exit. Turn right and continue 14 miles to the Welcome Creek trailhead parking area on the right.

**Hiking directions:** Cross the suspension bridge to the north side of Rock Creek, and head right along the banks of the creek. A short spur trail leads to the sandy beach at the base of the bridge. For a short distance, the trail follows Rock Creek downstream to a log bridge over Welcome Creek. After crossing, take the trail to the left (west), up canyon through the forest. The trail crosses several boulder fields separated by dense forest. There are some nettle plants which will make exposed legs tingle. At two miles, the trail crosses another log bridge over Welcome Creek. Just past the crossing is Cinnabar Cabin and Cinnabar Creek. This is our turnaround spot.

To hike further, the trail continues another 5 miles to Cleveland Mountain at 7,200 feet and the Bitterroot Divide. There is another mining ruin at Carron Creek, located 2 miles beyond Cinnabar Creek.

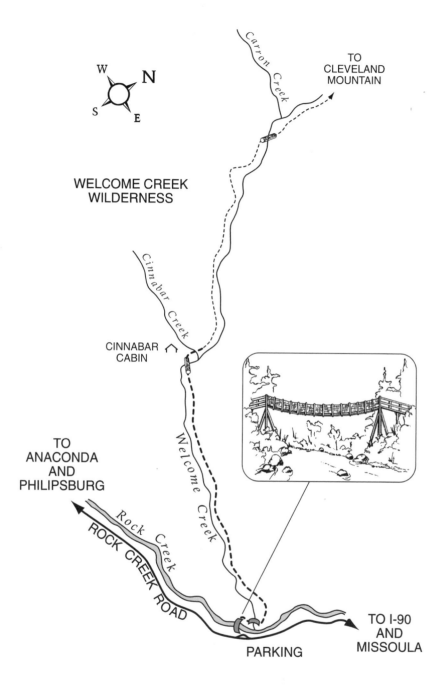

W N S E

Carron Creek

TO
CLEVELAND
MOUNTAIN

WELCOME CREEK
WILDERNESS

Cinnabar Creek

CINNABAR
CABIN

TO
ANACONDA
AND
PHILIPSBURG

Rock Creek

ROCK CREEK ROAD

Welcome Creek

TO I-90
AND
MISSOULA

PARKING

# WELCOME CREEK

# Other Day Hike Guidebooks

These books may be purchased at your local bookstore,
or they will be glad to order them.

**DAY HIKE BOOKS INC.**

# Notes